Scent Of Books

To amy, who smells of books & vintage libraries

Jyotsna P Katayaprath

Ukiyoto Publishing

Dedication

"For the two of them, home isn't a place. It is a person. And they are finally home."

To my children, Abhirami & Aswin, who have decided to hold on to one another, rest of their lives. Let you both fall in love with each other again and again, every time, everywhere...

Scent of Books- An invaluable gift from a mother to daughter.

This book is an outcome of a teenage girl's request to her mother, for the most beautiful, memorable, and precious gift on her wedding day. So, here is a mother recalling the most memorable events in their lives and intimate conversations they had had. The mother here outpours her emotions celebrating the special relationship between them. She captures the beads of wisdom and snapshots of common sense gathered from many lives' experiences.

Fragrant Dream

Anamika

My dream child, Unborn daughter
When the trickling drops of tears,
Make ripples in my heaving heart
I hear you lisp.
"Mother, take me out of this cover
for I want to taste this Life to the lees.
"Pardon me my child, too small is this world
for you to be born my darling.
oft I did wish to take you out.
But now
a threat of rain stops me
nightmare of the dark warns me
these thorns of life hurt me.
Why awaken those sleeping thoughts,
Just to be killed before they bloom?
Let you be my beautiful dream,
evidence to my existence
Let you sleep silently, swaddled,
forever in my heart.

(1996)

Contents

Aroma Of Words

"I hope that my daughter grows up empowered and doesn't define herself by the way she looks but by qualities that make her an intelligent, strong and responsible woman." — Isaiah Mustafa

I have far too many things to say to you, and I can't contain myself. Therefore, dear daughter, here I am, pouring my heart out to you with tears. I want to leave you with something you will cherish for a long time to come. You are hearing me, and it is your mother speaking to you, everything she wishes to convey to you in this lifetime. I am pelting you with words. Soak them up for years to come.

16 June,1997

Did the doctor mention that it's a girl? Or is it the longing of the heart to have a baby girl that echo from the heart? However, this is an overwhelming moment. Various thoughts, various emotions, traverse the mind. The news of my sis-in-law delivering a baby girl added joy to my happiness. Days of waiting began. I kept a watch of every single change happening to my body. My belly slowly blotted into a soft little bulge and I enjoyed pampering it generously on every single move. Yes, I am carrying a life, my soul, inside me. And very soon she will be out in the world, a tiny little miniature of mine, to add voice to my quiet and unengaging days.

Dear Amy

A mother's bond with her daughter is one of the most indissoluble one in the world. Something inside a woman shifts the moment she learns she's going to have a little miniature of hers. Call it hope, call it pleasure, call it love. The bottom line remains the same: a mother's emotional attachment to her daughter is aggressive. Is it ever a trapezium sort ? Yes, absolutely. But it's an exciting swing. You know, as a teenager, I vowed not to get married. My dream was to adopt a girl child, and I didn't know if a young girl could adopt. Four decades have passed since then. And then I met your father. The moment we decided to have a child, you know I started writing poems for my unborn daughter, Anamika, the unnamed. Yes, daughter, as I was undeniably sure that I will be blessed with a tiny cutie pie, a girl whom I can adorn like a Barbie doll.

Love

Amma

Scent of Candles and Cakes

"I see an incredible woman in you who knows what she wants out of life. Your ambition is admirable, and I'm grateful to be able to watch you grow!"

Dear Amy

Did you know that I became a mother for the first time at the age of thirteen? Flabbergasted, I guess! Yes, let me elucidate...

One evening when I got home, your grandparents said that we have some guests staying with us for a while. A family that has become so bonded with us even though we were no blood relations. One of your grandpa's acquittances had got transferred from Kannur to Kozhikode. Her husband, left herself and their eight months old son at ours. They were accompanied by an aunt to care for the infant. Initial inhibitions proved transitory and very soon, I saw myself playing the role of Cuckoo's mother in all my leisure time. When he started to lisp, he called me "Mole" like everyone else. Even before he turned two years old, they were transferred back to the native. Back then was a void silently surging in.

I grew into a mother again soon after my 18th birthday. After my graduation and before joining Masters, I became a mother to the daughter of your grandma's colleague's daughter. I fed the one-year-old girl, put her to sleep, and played with her, until her mom was back from school. Then finally I became a mother biologically at the age of twenty-six. Ever since I found out that I was carrying a life within, I began manifesting for a baby girl. Since then, I kept writing letters and poems in my diary addressed to that baby to be born. All those were superscribed "to Anamika, my love"- for that baby girl to be born. Finally, after three days of pain, she took birth on a sunny morning in the month of February, and today she's turned eighteen!

Happy birthday Amy!

To my INFJ Girl, from your ESFP Mom

Dear,

Welcome to the most beautiful

world of womanhood. Obviously, I laugh at myself wishing you so, because you've always made me feel yourself to be womanlier when compared to me. The way you frown and scold like an elder sister watching my frowny face-" this is what I don' t like in you. Behave like a grown up..."-

Yes, at times you are more of a mentor to me...I still cherish the wish you expressed when I commented that I'd gift you a library on your wedding day. You replied, yes, but I also want you to write me a book for my special day. Hand it over to me wrapped in a colorful gift paper painted gold and silver, on the day instead of covering me up in yellow metal... You put me in tears when you wished me happy fathers' day, cuddling on my lap, last year. When I said, go wish your father the same, you said, "Aren't you more of a father to me?" I feel, everything about you is at times out of this world, but I will always love and respect it. I promise to support you in whatever you decide to do in life because I know it is your journey. You had been telling me you would be a writer and a traveler. I wouldn't be surprised. Whatever you do and wherever you go, I will wrap my arms around your hip and cling my little finger to yours like we always do when we move around, rubbing your cheeks on mine, like I do right now. I will always walk by you tied up by that invisible, sacred string. I'm not troubled about you, because wherever you are, I'm sure of what you are doing, even when you are unsure. I will let you do whatever your heart desires. I will support you and guide you and give you all the knowledge that I have because I want you to flourish in whatever you love.

You will always be safe, protected, and be loved, with the grace of that magic only two of us know. Go explore, be daring, be undaunted, be spirited-because you are meant to dream, discover, to construct, to acquire, and to involve. You are meant to be that unique YOU. with love n prayers

yours
jack O 'lantern

Scent Of Vintage Libraries

"Rivers know this: there is no hurry. We shall get there some day."
A.A. Milne

5 February, 1998

I was in labour for three nights and two days, before you were born. I had early contractions and my doctor asked for an immediate admission in the hospital. I lay biting my lips so that no-one could hear me groan. When the vacuum suction failed for the first time I shuddered at the loud burst, praying that my girl wouldn't panic at the thunderous noise. You were then sucked out. I looked at the enormous clock behind me. It showed 11:54 AM. The cord was cut and you were wiped in soft cloth. I heard your cry something like I have heard only in movies. You cried,"lleeeeyy...lleeeeyyy" I smiled. I watched the pediatrician examine you. I didn't feel the pain of labour nor the stitches made around the genitals. I twisted my head and looked at you as the doctor placed you near my bed. You cried, and I wept in joy.

When you were born, I could smell the sweet, inviting aroma of old books. Your dusky soft velvety skin scented of vintage libraries. Nothing in life had prepared me for the overwhelming meet with you. Words aren't just enough to describe the inexplicable love I felt for you at that moment. Ever since that day, my life wasn't the same.

 Love

Amma

8 February, 1999

Dear Amy

Today as you turn one, I'm super excited. You are growing up with me. I guess you like this green floral dress. It's of your type, I'm sure. Past twelve months I've been keenly trying to learn you. The meanings of your smiles, cries, frowns and silence. Your moods and features. Your paternal grandma and myself has together prepared the sadya. Your maternal grandparents, uncles and aunts will be here soon. I think you are feeling a sort of importance today as I see you so extraordinarily content and happy. Your spirit seems unusually high this day. Let you be happy and smiling always my sweetheart, I pray. As you position for the Photograph, I grasp dreams in your eyes. Long years ahead. Yes, we will grow together, you and me, daughter and mother at times, and friends at other times.

I often used to wonder what if dreams made no meaning in my life. Yes, the space between dreams and reality were getting papery. Twilight set new dimensions to everything seen before. I dreamt, and I became the dream myself. As it is said intentions squashed into words have magical powers, so are the dreams crammed into thoughts, and thereby extracted into realities. Law of attraction, may be. Pondering over, I realize everything we come across do run into us for a reason. Some moments stay, some pass. Yet some others take a journey back through the road that wanted wear.

Ammamma always had tips enough to advise us. She had asked us to move forward in small paces. She had encouraged us to do what we have to do, but little by little. She insisted not to think too much about the future or what may become tomorrow, as whatever is designed for us will come seeking us. We just have to seek them on the go, she had said. You understand? Advance step by step. Take a step and then stop. Rest a little. Take time to praise yourself, because unless and until we appreciate ourselves, nobody else will do so! Take another step. And then another. At this, even without notice, your steps will grow more and more and take different turns. And the time will come when you can plan the future without regrets and dissatisfaction.

It was Ammamma's prayer to take you to Guruvayoor temple on every birthday of yours. An ardent lover of lord Krishna, I have seen ammamma weep in front of lord Krishna's idol seeking good health and prosperity for her granddaughter. She also expressed her gratitude, for all those she had, with eyes wet and smiling, in front of him. So, we were there, the three of us, at the temple celebrating your day. You loved sitting at the koothambalam for hours and watching the hustle and bustle around. You would open your eyes wide in awe and wonder watching the elephants so close. Strange people around at their best temple attire and jewelry kept you engaged. And we used to sit there watching you pick up the red manjadi beads scattered on the ground, and tot around blabbering in a world of your own. Your innocent cuteness would invite anyone to gift you with the Prasad, maybe the bananas, payasam or unniyappams offered to the lord. Once we were even taken to the Oottupura (dining where holy Prasad is served) by a stranger, who insisted us to leave only after having the noon meal Prasad, which was to be served soon. I was awestruck wondering how only we were picked by him to this place from among thousands, and where an ocean of humans was waiting to get a chance to enter in! Yes, as grandma had always said, what you seek is seeking you too.

Dear daughter,

Mark this thought of your grandma as the tag line of life. Don't ever let fear paralyze your vision. Live your dreams dear. For this, you must of course move out of your comfort zones. Be prepared to face risks in your life and once you are ready you will find you blossoming. On the move many distractions may pop up. But have courage enough to discard them. Find that extra dose of inspiration from those people you love. Their support will surely fuel your journey forward. So, if you dream to write your first book, plan your pages for each day. Set your clock and priority time. And when you wake up, you'll know that it's time to fire up your imagination. Set deadline and track your progress. Tell your love who I know will hold you accountable. Be sure to give him the right to provide an adequately operative twinge if you think of missing your day's goal! Howzat? Simply push yourself to action when you feel like doing and when you don't. And dear don't forget to appreciate and celebrate your achievements. 'Coz, you deserve it. Remember you are not alone in your journey. There is somebody with you now to walk on your side along with you to support you, and of course, we are here. Yes, dreams do come true dear.

Now you scent of books and the moonlight...

Love
Amma

Odour Of Magic-Wand

"Ah, what happiness it is to be with people who are all happy,
to press hands, press cheeks, smile into eyes".
Katherine Mansfield

Often, I am reminded of those women of your life, who co-staged you at certain junctures of life's journey. Girija vallyamma, Shobha Chechi, Jalaja aunty, Indu vallyamma: all who entered straight into your heart at certain points of your infancy and cared for you unconditionally. These where the people you loved being with in my absence. Then there were your paternal aunts, whom you played with, danced, and sang like a cuckoo bird. You've always been a shy person who had little communication with individuals and have had handful relationships. But, based on the few interactions, and the companionship you've had with these, I can say with conviction that, despite your coyness, a touch, or a hug from these women of your life, could put you to sleep.

There was a time in my life when I badly wanted to take a break. I felt too empty then like an evening bloom. I knew my days were full of beauty, and enchantment but I couldn't find solace. I wanted to declutter myself or rather unplug from the weary days around. That's what lead to our Thirunavaya days. You were an infant then and I took a maid along with me to take care of you in my absence, or when I was away for work. I remember you crying your heart out one day, whispering under your sobs, "I don't want to be left alone with dark-skinned Kamalamma, Amma." Kamalamma was the lady who had come all the way from Wayanad to Thirunavaya just to take care of you. I very soon noticed that the lady was becoming a burden for me. I had to make food, bed and a living for this lady for no reason! Because, you loved being with the house owner's wife, who was quite fair and graceful. Kamalamma's presence appeared to be an expression of discomfort for you. I was embarrassed by your attitude towards her every time you cried at her presence. Your misconceptions with complexion worried me. I wanted to erase the thoughts of colorism, the principle of treating lighter skinned with a higher regard than those with darker skin. But it was not your fault. It was what the society fed human brains with. However, Kamalamma too didn't much bother about your indifferent attitude towards her. Her only concern was what if I send her back to native!!! Obviously, I had to see her off very soon. Later I realized how unhappy you have felt with your body weight when people around started to judge your body. I could sense your anxiety, and it made me upset. But then your passion, the hobby that you developed slowly pulled you away from those negative comments. The little you were strong willed beyond my perceptions.

Today, these yellow tinted pages of dog-eared Harry Potter series, bear testimony to that musty smell of yours during those times. Certain days when you smile at the moon, you scented the vintage musk. Everything about you scented vintage bookstores. You were all books and coffee mugs as you grew older. In the wintry mornings you smelt drizzling dew, and the twilights propagated the aroma of roses infused potpourris, and fragrant candles.

The shimmering stars in the night sky excited you. You kept awake gazing at the sky for hours. I read a sea of thoughts rushing through the tiny you. You lay your shoulders on me like a bookmark upon the unread pages of life. I realised that you are the one writing the pages of my life, and adding on designs to my destiny since then.

Love

Amma

Fragrance Of Misty Mornings

"If you change the way you look at things, the things you look at change." Wayne Dyer

It was when you turned six that we decided to have a second baby. You may laugh out loud when I say that I loved babies and wanted a whole lot of them around me, girls most of them, wailing and puking and pooing in and out!!! When we declared that you are going to be an elder sister you did wish that hopefully it could be a baby boy so that you need not share your toys!!! That birthday at the abode of Lord Krishna, at the Sanctum sanctorum, you touched my belly softly and said, "Amma, It's of course little Krishna, my Unni inside you." Later sitting at the hospital bed, cuddling the new born you said, " see didn't I tell you it's going to be my cute bunny brother!!"

Unni was a heavy baby, and the tiny you, used to literally trip holding him! But you never let him down. Your elders believed that you were always near him, as you were envious of him, seeing him lay near me and feed on me. But later you have proved that it was only out of pure and innocent sisterly affection that you possessed for that cute little bunny, that you never left my side! You shared all you toy with your naughty brother. You didn't complain even when he broke all your well-kept toys, one by one. I enjoyed the bond you kept with him and the way you loved and cared for him.

Though I wanted many more babies, your grandma warned me that I should bear more only if I am capable of taking care of many more. Since Unni's birth was a bit byzantine I too decided to have another thought. At a point I even thought of adopting babies for which both of you threw a furious frown at me. Dear, today as I watch the two of you, my heart fills with love and content. I know both of you will be there for each other lifelong. The way you share and care for each other leaves my overwhelming heart at peace. This sibling love is a bliss. I know you both are irritating, annoying and what not, at times, to each other, but, sure, if there occurs any difficulty in life, protect one another.

Yes, this sharing demonstrates your concern and consideration for each other. Your friendliness, your kindness and concern will touch one another's heart when you share anything. Let you treat each other well and cherish one another. But remember to share everything including your troubles. When you share your worries, like you do with me, you will feel a bit relieved. I don't have to tell you that being a listener is one of the best qualities you can inculcate. Listen to one another with your heart. Be bold enough to talk about your concerns to each other.

Both of you be the kind of persons that people can share their problems with. Be protective of one another. Let this amazing bond remain the same even after years have passed by, I pray, 'coz both of you are the most precious happenings in my life.

Love from Amma

Smell Of Desperateness

"When you're at the end of your rope, tie a knot and hold on."
–Theodore Roosevelt

I can only reminisce that distressing Monday morning with a sigh of remorse. We were all at your fathers to mourn the demise of your paternal grandmother, when I received a call asking me to be present at the capital city the very next day, for some important work for the department. I had no other choice but to leave you there and rush to Trivandrum. Back home, after a couple of days, what I saw was quite alarming. You were there, a puny little thing, buried under a bundle of clothes burning with fever and your cute little face all swelled up. Amma said your doctor had asked her to get you shifted to a hospital for further investigation. My vision blurred; muscles froze. Eyes welled up. When I regained consciousness, I found myself at the doctors with you cuddled on to my bosom. That morning after great grandma's death you had hit your forehead over a rusted tap, and the wound had become septic. I shuddered at the realization that I have carelessly missed your TT vaccine of 10 years. I sat with my head lowered at the doctors, at his acquisition of being so scatter-brained. He prescribed you antibiotics for a week, which literally kept you glued to the bed. But very soon the swelling on the face turned out to become a large puss filled acne on your forehead. At the next visit he said that he is going to perform a minor surgery to get the puss out and dress it up. I looked around. Your father had left us there and gone to attend a meeting at the office. I felt so helpless when the nurse pulled you away from me. I couldn't watch them cut open the puss-filled bulb. I turned my face away from you. But suddenly you started screaming and shaking your head. Finally, the doctor decided to conduct the surgery at the theatre after a couple of days. That was more fearsome and unbearable for me. I felt guilty and cursed myself. I couldn't imagine the sight you at the surgery. I cried my heart out.

Finally, the destined day arrived. Somehow your father could make it to be with me on the day. I was allowed to be with you till you were taken to the surgery. I couldn't bear the sight of tiny you in that oversized green hospital gown. I wept in silence. The anesthetist called me up and asked a few questions for which I replied mechanically. Then he explained the procedure. I didn't hear a word. I saw only you, your fearful eyes, and your distorted, tight lips. Your requesting looks pierced my heart. Your cold arms clinging to my neck. I felt so pathetic. A sob of grief escaped my throat. As the door of the surgery closed behind me, I closed my eyes. I went void within. I was away from the world around.

Five hours had passed when the nurse came out and asked for your bystander. I rushed in to find you barely conscious, blabbering for water. Doctor asked me to be with you at the post operative ward. That was the concession given for the tiny you, and your helpless mother. He also warned me not to give you water for a couple of hours. I was with the semi-conscious you , and a handful of howling humans around us. That was like being in a world away from earth. A hell like laboratory where humans are being experimented with.

To my relief you gained consciousness in another couple of hours. The doctor smiling, asked me to buy you your favourite dish. You smiled at him; your lashes still wet. I too smiled, painfully, my eyes darkened due to long sobs. I held you close to my heart. I took your pale, cold, fingers towards my lips. You smelled of wet earth. Seeing you smile I realized, it was the most beautiful moment that had ever happened to me. The whole world cuddled into a tiny you, and the scent of earth lured me towards my world.

Every alternate day I had to take you to the hospital for dressing up the wound on your forehead. You were recovering fast. I pulled my eyes away from you when the nurse cleaned up the wound and applied medicine. I couldn't bear the sight of your sobbing mouth and pathetic looks. But within a couple of weeks, you regained your health and started off with new pranks. The Naughty-You moments were back again.

Today while sitting here watching this independent you... I understand, may be those traumatic experiences that we lived through had made me hesitant to leave you at the care of anybody else then. Where ever I went, I carried you along with me. When I had to make those official journeys again, I left you with Amma, because she was the only one, I had faith in, to be with you, after me. Thus, we grew together, crying laughing, shouting, yelling, and pranking. YOU and ME, WE, US. One soul in different bodies. I kiss you, and you now smell of the Twilight sky.

Dear

Life at times may play such odd games with us. Never lose your heart. Try to turn every hard moment of the life to a glory. I always wish to see you with this infectious cheerfulness of yours. This will help you act better and preserve it for longer. When everything goes topsy-turvy, have patience and courage. Engrave the words "this too shall pass" on your heart and soul and sinew. You are bold enough to overcome anything, I know. It only takes a moment to lose everything that we have hoarded in a life time. Have courage enough to start all over. Remember, nothing can destroy you sweetheart! Always dream big and believe in making it a reality. Success, is the result of determination, dedication, perseverance, self-confidence and willpower. Above all what you need is to have immense belief in yourself and the ability to never give up on your dreams even after going through numerous failures.

Love

Amma

Here 'N Now: Scent Of The Moment

"I have great respect for the past. If you don't know where you've come from, you don't know where you're going. I have respect for the past, but I'm a person of the moment. I'm here, and I do my best to be completely centered at the place I'm at, then I go forward to the next place." Maya Angelou

Whether I made the right decision in marrying your dad is still up for debate. As far as I am concerned, there are no perfect choices; there are only just choices, and we, those who make the choices, should drive them forward carefully. There is always the possibility of disagreements when two individuals hail from two different environments with entirely different personalities. However, listening to each other makes life easier. Effective communication turns out to be the villain in many relationships. We will be able to sort out things tactfully if we take the time to speak to each other and ponder over the events. To err is human, forgive divine. The more we blame each other when things don't work out well, the more hatred and contempt will build. Put yourself at ease and discuss the situation calmly. Together, try to come up with solutions. Be communicative. A successful partnership is built on effective communication. I have often felt that this is where your dad and I stammer. When I feel depressed or emotional, I often try to connect with people through words or letters. In spite of this, your father had often remained silent like a sage. Eventually, I stopped expecting it and began accepting it as part of who he is. Our contentment and happiness come from only remembering the happy moments together and from only thinking of the positives about each other. It's what keeps us going, now two decades and a half later!

So dear daughter, communicate. Don't wait for the other to begin with the conversation. Speak your heart out and be at ease. Expect less and accept more. For this is what a partnership is all about; finding perfections among all those imperfections. It's easy to let go people from our lives. But very difficult to maintain relationships. So, Forgive. Because flaws and goodness is inherent in every human. We are the Devil, and the God. And it is possible that every hopeless person gets transformed. Let's leave it to time. You may feel drained at times but there are ways to refill and recharge you. Seek your own ways, and you will meet up once!

Despite the fact that money can provide material comforts in life, it cannot provide us with happiness. It cannot get you people. Our lives are more peaceful and satisfying when we are committed to honesty and faithfulness. What hinders this is replaying the past, and overthinking of future. Past is past, and rewinding those unpleasant experience of the past will only add on to your anger and sorrows. Future is yet to come. Obsessed with how it's going to be will only increase your anxiety. So dear daughter, stay in the present moment. Make the most out of it. Make it beautiful. Undoubtedly, life is a wonderful opportunity to learn and grow, a wonderful gift. Live your life to the fullest.

Dear Amy,

Yesterday, I watched you build a house using the blocks. Every time a block fell down, very patiently you picked it up and kept on trying. I was so surprised that you never felt tired of trying. Yes dear, in the course of life you may fall many a times. But keep the same spirit as you did the other day. Never get tired of getting up every time you fall. Your ability to overcome the negative emotions and defeats will be greatly enhanced by learning to embrace failure and setbacks as an inevitable part of life. Battle with your own failures and blunders, can teach you things about how to improve yourself.

Understand that failure is by no means uncommon. Just like you, many others are making mistakes as well. Our lives are moving too quickly, as the requirements are piling up one on top of another. It may seem like you'll never be able to catch up. Learn to control the sadness and negativity you generally experience at this point; you must investigate what transpired. Consider the circumstances that occurred. Ruminate the positive and negative aspects of what happened. What went right and what went wrong. You will surely gain valuable insights and a greater sense of self-awareness by responding to thoughts of this kind.

In the journey of life, you may endure a variety of emotions like shame, disappointment, identity crisis, feeling useless and unimportant, thinking you have nothing to contribute, and even believing others are superior to you. You know, we could certainly go on and on about this since, for some reason, we humans love to criticize ourselves, especially in light of all our past unsuccessful attempts and mistakes.

You risk harming your mental health if you allow these thoughts and feelings to run amok in your head. So, just like if you were getting ready to fight someone else, you're going to plan your attack on these feelings before they manifest.

So, Think, Acknowledge, Act, and Repeat. Find out your rejuvenation style. This is the rudimentary step; bounce back from falls.

With love

Amma

Fragrance Of Love

"Okay, life's a fact, people do fall in love, people do belong to each other, because that's the only chance anybody's got for real happiness."
—Paul (George Peppard), from Breakfast at Tiffany's

Do you abscond from

people for fear of love? Afraid of falling in love, afraid of being loved? If yes, you must have experienced this too. Those who walk away from you, as if they aren't aware of it! Have you noticed them? How gentle they are! They smile at you in the most beautiful manner! And through this smile, they can make you believe that you are the whole reason for your limitations. They have that potential that just by being with them, they will manifest you to bend yourself with guilt. They are the ones who slowly drift away from you, when schemas are accomplished, or when they feel you are not up to them. You might have kept them close to your heart for a short period of time, or perhaps even for a long time, without expecting anything in return, out of the basic human feelings of love, compassion, concern and care. You might have sheltered them like a temporary motel. But for those people, it's just a momentary settlement before they reach their goal! Just keep a watch over watch and you will see them forget everything about you and getting fascinated in new hubs. They recognize that you are a wasteland for them to grow in, and you realize it too. All the while, you will have taught your mind not to settle down for momentary happiness. Dear, know that those who drift apart are definitely cowards who lack self-esteem. They will continue to do so, with anyone, anywhere. But one thing is certain; in flashes of realization, they will only be thinking about you. They will be waiting for a sign from you to return to your shelter. They will keep their eyes on you for a resolution. This compulsion is beyond arguments and you will know their attitude!!! But by then, you will be many light-years away from humans, afraid of being loved, afraid of falling in love.

So dear, remove yourself from the state to avoid such scenes. Either leave the place or remain uninvolved while dealing exploiters. Hale and hearty relationships comprise give and take. i.e., if we offer support, we receive support, too. Also, make sure you have enough emotional energy to meet your own desires. There is nothing incorrect with accepting support. But be careful as all favors are not benevolent.

Love

Amma

Scent Of Happiness

"The secret of happiness, you see, is not found in seeking more, but in developing the capacity to enjoy less" — *Socrates*

Dear Daughter

Today I was watching you tot around with your rattling turtle. I found you gathering your tiny assets on the go and place it carefully in the turtle belly storage. I noticed that it was a broken piece of crystal bangle, a colourful sticky note, two pencils, a sketch pen, and a rubber ball. You looked excited at the rattling sound of the turtle. I could see a sweet awe in your bright eyes and a smile of happiness at the corner of your lips. My heart leapt up in an inexplicable joy. Every time I saw you content and happy like this I feel so filled up.

Dear, Happiness as you see is something that comes your way on the move. Never miss it. Gather it unfailingly as you move around. Like you find happiness in this broken piece of crystal bangle, try to find it in every little wonder that you come across. Happiness always comes as a piecemeal. Take it in slow phase. Devour it. Relish it. Taste it. In years to come you may thus be able to find happiness in every trivial happening of life. Remember, every day is a wonder. Dear, happiness as you see is relative. What I consider a matter of happiness may not seem to be so, to you. So always try to be at your good and flourish. Your propensity for experiencing various moods decides your emotional balance, thereby instilling satisfaction and happiness in you. Try to distract yourself enough with constant activity to maintain a mostly pleasant existence. Practice techniques to keep all anxieties away. As you grow older, don't forget to evaluate and self-introspect your days activities every night before sleep. This will well allow you to make modifications for the next. Let your being itself be a reason for your happiness. In the course of time, life may get busy. But manage your time accordingly to lower your stress. Take time to sit and ruminate your beautiful moments. Do all those activities that you enjoy. Let you yourself be the most loving and valued friend of yourself. This will help you boost your self-esteem. Be resilient so that you can cop up with ups and downs in the life. Get creative and turn every bad experience into something worthwhile. But never hide your feelings. Talk and share your emotions with your most loved ones. As long as Amma is with you, and after, I will be there to listen you, and support you whenever you trip off.

Love

Amma

Scent Of Books

"When I look back, I am so impressed again with the life-giving power of literature. If I were a young person today, trying to gain a sense of myself in the world, I would do that again by reading, just as I did when I was young." – Maya Angelou

As you grew older you smelt of books. Sometimes old, sometimes new. At times I opened you up, pulled you towards my nostrils and inhaled you to the fullest. Other times you scented like morning dew or fresh earth. But most of the times it felt as if you smelt the old and pale *Mills 'N Boons* or *Famous Five* that adorned my study, during my college days. I loved the way you loved me gift you books on your birthdays. No wonder why you became a bookaholic on growing up. I secretly watched you converse with the characters. Sometimes I laughed a little listening to your love talks with those fictitious crushes of yours. You loved, you quarreled, and even broke-up with them. And on the other side, I kept reading you untiringly. The more I read you your branches spread into immense new pages. You broke yourself into infinity and i found myself fumbling around in the corners. You were an ocean of thoughts. I was never able to keep my pace with you.

Today as you move out leaving more and more for me to explore, I skim through your titles to catch up with you. I watched you get excited at everything. A tiny bit of dark chocolate, a pair of white vintage curtains, pale crystals with green veins, or a book of your choice; all could leave you speechless. Then I read your astonished eyes. A tint of Mahagony upon the white moon; yes, your eyes roll in wonder. Then you smell of vanilla and mango. I wake up and find that the bus to Kovilkandi has left Vengalam gate. That puny little thing is no more an infant. I find a grown-up lady seated near me. Most sophisticated and elegant in every gesture of hers.

Dear Daughter

Do you have the least guess that my days and nights are all orbiting around you!!!

Today is a beautiful day, and as I sit here this dewy dawn, covered with a blanket of mild chillness, listening to the morning drizzles upon petals and leaves, how content I feel for living to the fullest! Yes, I express my deepest gratitude for this in explicably magnificent morning. The singing birds, chirping squirrels, dancing white flowers, the still silvery sky, dew drops wetting my nose tip, and my turbulent mind overwhelmed with a rush of emotions! I understand that these magnificent moments are getting lost in the ocean of infinite time and will never come back again except as memories silently singing in my subconscious mind. Yes dear, life is beautiful and like any other beautiful thing, it's difficult to maintain its beauty, as at time and again we will have to groom it to keep it flowing with all its charm and glow. So, keep your self-confidence and self-love, have immense belief in yourself and this beautiful life. I wish you stand out in the crowd, throw out your lights and glow, at every chance that come your way. Simply shine out loud! In the course of life don't forget to give each other the space to grow, to be yourself, to exercise your diversity. When the two of you give space to each other space, it's a give and take of novel ideas, openness, dignity, happiness, healing, and satisfaction. People say you are made for each other. But I would say, you are each other; You him, He, you!

Smell Of Healing

*"Forgiveness does not change the past, but it does enlarge the future." – **Paul Boese***

Bedtime stories were those that had kept us busy all night. I used to snore even before you fell asleep. Stories and poems never lulled you to sleep, but kept you awake, astonished, and with eyes wide open you used to sit alert waiting for the next. Today when I saw you short fuse, I was reminded of that Friday evening years ago. I was back from the school and you weren't at the veranda waiting for me unlike the other days. I called you by your name but you didn't reply. Then I heard your heavy anklet tinkling behind the kitchen. When I reached behind what I saw was the tiny you, with a heavy billhook, rushing behind *Achachan's* pet kitten. I was shocked. I couldn't even think could have happened if you fell down with the weapon in your arms. So, with a velvet tread, very stealthily, I reached behind you and caught hold of the knife. You said you were angry that *Achacha* paid more attention to his kittens more than you. That night my story for you was about a little boy who had a bad temper, and whose father gave him a bag of nails asking him to hammer a nail into the back of the fence, every time he lost his temper. The first day, the boy had driven around forty nails into the fence. However, it was a difficult task. Over the next few weeks, he learned to control his anger. He understood that holding his temper was easier than driving nails into the fence. So, the number of nails hammered daily gradually dwindled down.

Finally, the day came when there weren't any nails at all. Then the father suggested that he now pull out one nail for each day that he was able to hold his temper. The days passed and the boy was finally able to tell his father that all the nails were pulled out. The father took his son to the fence. He said, "You have pulled the nails but look at the holes in the fence. The fence will never be the same. When you say things in anger, they leave a scar just like this one. You can hurt people with your words and actions. It won't matter how many times you say 'I'm sorry'. The scar will remain."

Dear, today I was reminded of this incident seeing you break out emotionally at a trivial happening. If you had a second thought this could have been avoided. Dear daughter, a verbal wound is as bad as a physical one. Only few people would array to have irascibility as a quality. Being easily offended has consequences for both your physical and mental health, in addition to making people around you always tread carefully so as not to set off your temper.

Try to concentrate on calming techniques like deep breathing when you notice clear indications that your anger is rising. It might also help to control your anger to support your breathing with soothing remarks. To avoid an outburst and the detrimental effects that come with it, keep doing this exercise until your anger has been calmed. Have a second thought before you react. Life is beautiful, and so is all the lovely people in your life. It's easy to ruin these precious assets easily. But remember mending leaves a scar. Better avoid the situations that leave a scar.

Love

Amma

Fragrance Of Freedom

"I have found both freedom and safety in my madness; the freedom of loneliness and the safety from being understood, for those who understand us enslave something in us." — Kahlil Gibran

Dear daughter, let me remind you that the secret of happiness is freedom and the pathway towards freedom is courage. Remember, there must be no particular reason for one to be happy. Just choose to be happy every single day and there you go! Never allow the negativity of others daunt you. Once you allow it to gnaw your thoughts, unhappiness will invade you. So just enjoy everything, every moment. Rain, Snow, Sun, Moon, Wind, Grass, Flower, and Sky anything that touches your heart, will show you what happiness is! When you feel low and unhappy, just affirm yourself that all days are happy days. Feel the bliss of life. While the presence of some makes you happy, the absence of some others too make you happy! How else to mark our joys here but with this free bird life! Dear, So, disable all those default buttons from life, and design your own, independent life. You start to live, the moment you realize that this life is not something that happens by chance, but is the sum total of each person's choices. Dear, if you are able to face anything that comes your way, with such a positive attitude, life will seem feather like. Nothing will daunt you. When you see people around you getting recognized, you appreciate.

You won't feel any sort of unbearable pain, but happiness. Change the auto mode of instant acquaintances to manual mode and check the review option. Leave it there. It's possible to stay "out of the box" to toxic unhealthy relationships with a smile and be assertive approaching them. Leaving the hoax of misidentifying it for love, enjoying to the fullest the sweetness of tender friendships without unnecessary expectations, so that you float and fly like a fluffy feather, weightless. Inoculate warmth and transparency in all healthy relationships. The moment we start thinking of the others, passivity begins to affect us. So, what are you waiting for. Sieve out all that remains undigested. Clear your throat and throw away whatever is trapped in within. Fit a cool filter inside your ear, and carry a fire-breathing tornado on the tip of your pen So, Chin up, Eyes straight, Steady pace and keep smiling...

Love

Amma

Musk Of Humans

*"There should be no boundaries to human endeavor. We are all different. **However bad life may** seem, there is always something you can do, and succeed at. While there's life, there is hope."*
—Stephen Hawking, The Theory of Everything

Dear Daughter

Don't you remember your upper primary days, when you were curiously watching the long travels of about an inch long Ant, carrying a grain nearly fifty time it's weight? You used to whisper to them and express your wonder at their untiring enthusiasm. Dear, just like these ants, we also feel high and rewarded when everything comes out well after a hard try. It makes us feel better.

But in life sometimes it may seem like you've been trying tirelessly for no reason. Then you may get frustrated soon and you may feel like you still aren't nearly where you want to be. You may even start blaming yourself and everyone around you. You may think "why the hell should I try again?"

This is when disappointment pops up in your head. You think of quitting. You may feel fed-up of putting so much time and energy into things that never seem to come your way. But let me tell you, this is the moment to push even harder. Keep moving even if you stumble. Always walk forward even if you are waking slow.

Dear Amy

You know, I am laughing my heart out as I write this. How childish I have behaved with you at times!!!And every time, I remember, you would roll your eyes and say, "Whatever, Mom, that was so mean and rude of you!" But I know, when we fight, it's all out of love and the possessiveness that we have for each other. I have many times pretended as I can't hear you when you tell me to cook for you or help you out with other works. But dear, it's not because I am at that disrespect spectrum, but just because my weak body and mind wouldn't support me to. Many a times my physical and mental weaknesses have turned out to be challenging for you. Hope you could understand it now as a grown up. I am sorry for all those. I've always been a little selfish about you. I've secretly held you toward me tightly and said to myself "Mine!" I know this isn't a good thing as I have time and again been insecure, and kept controlling you. You must have felt think you are suffocated at my behaviour. But time fled by I understood that it had only helped us to hurt one another and to wear out trust, respect, and love. So dear daughter, when someone hurt you, write it down in sand where winds of forgiveness can erase it away. But, when someone does something good for you, engrave it in rock where no wind can ever erase it. Try to find goodness in every human you meet. Let alone their goodness touch you. Don't value the materials you hoard in your life. But value the goodness of people you have in your life.

Haven't you heard the story of a little boy who told about a fight between two wolves inside him? When somebody asked him about the winner among the two, the grandpa had replied that the wolf whom the boy had fed, won. Yes sweetheart, it's up to us to decide what to take in. The more we nurture the goodness within our own hearts, the more we are able to recognize the good in others. But if we fail to foster the goodness within ourselves, we will not be able to see the good in others. But rather, will always be searching out their faults and flaws. So, stop judging people, that you don't find time to love them.

Love

Amma

Smell Of Earth

"You have pierced my soul, I'm half agony half hope. I've loved none but you." –Jane Austen

I have always found stories during my travels. I find those pecking at my doorstep like a long-awaited guest. Like every other guest, I invite them into my little closet, where they perch, lay eggs and then rest until I let them fly away. So, every time I feel like talking to you, I go to those stories, and listen them closely without any judgement. Then in a happy state of mind I start conversions with my thoughts.

Today let me tell you about Pooja. It was during my journey to the Ajantha caves last summer, that I met Pooja. Pooja and I got close very soon, though after the initial inhibitions. And then she became a story herself! She had then told me about her love for Manjeet and how she had paid attention to things like him being a good cook and wearing smart attires. As per the words of Pooja, he had all the qualities that she wanted in a perfect partner. But unfortunately, she delayed in letting him know her feelings for him when they were together. That had once made her life difficult with him. It was not until she started living with him, she realised that perfect partnership means accepting the imperfections of each other. The moment she realised this, she says, she was surprised and stunned that every little detail that she always wished for had manifested in the form of her partner, and they now adore one another for being themselves.

Dear Amy

On this Big day of yours I'd like to remind you that a marriage partnership is a lot like any architecture: without a good foundation, they'll crumble. When something in the building disfunction, you don't build a new building, or shift from the same, but you find out the error and change the part that's not functioning. When the faucet drips, you don't start mopping the floor before you fix the leak. In other words, no matter how much deep you'll have to dig, it's important to get to the root of a problem. Rectify the problem and proceed. Listen to each other and understand what each other is trying to say before you reply. I know you both keep that emotional intimacy in your relationship. I know how much both of enjoy the feeling that you're really understood and loved by one another even with all your imperfections. And this deep sense of knowing, that you are being swaddled by heart and soul by someone who really matters to you, is the best part of being in a relationship. In the chase of happiness, you will naturally follow relationships that are not centered on your joy. There is no limit to the number of relationships you can maintain and do so well. When you are an expression of joy, if you do not worry about meeting the expectations of others, they will want to be around you anyway. It is imperative that you shift your life focus from hunting happiness to expressing joy, if you want relationships to work on all levels. Allow your relationship to be strong enough to withstand life's challenges. This is because your bond is so strong that problems can actually bring you closer together. In quest for true love, the couple may almost immediately feel brave, wanting to know and be known regardless of the outcome. After all, love is founded on the gradual development of trust, respect, and honesty. Nothing beats falling deeply and profusely in love with someone. True love spans oceans and towers over mountains. It finds every nook and cranny of our hearts and fills them with the most wonderful joys. If we open ourselves completely to this sensory experience, we can be gripped by the massiveness of love.

Dear, however, both of you may not always be in agreement with each other and that there may be some unnecessary tension between the two of you. but, take this tension as an experience of companionship, friendship and love.

Here you will have to respond to each other instead of reacting. Understand, humans are the consolidation of every experience they live through.

So, love each other, care for each other, and understand. Here the happiness of both the partners matters a lot. Improve each other every moment. When both of you aren't taking things smoothly, just keep silent and sit apart. Then take deep breaths, relax and come back to say, "I am sorry, I didn't mean to be so critical and hurt you. You are great.

The time is just not ideal for us, that's all. Let's sit down and sort things out together." This talking is important, you know, because, both of you are so good, so sweet and so special to me!

Lots of love

Amma

Odour Of Fire

"Everything you can imagine is real."
Pablo Picasso

Dear Son,

On this happiest day of yours, I give you the most expensive gift I ever can. That is, My life, My Amy. Do Love and accept her as I do. She may sound weird and act stubborn and tough at times, but do love and accept her as I do. She is not perfect and she may even act silly, but she is my daughter, do love and accept her as unconditionally as I do. She is the precious thing that my hand has ever held, and I have nothing dearer to offer you, except my life, and so I offer you my life, My Amy. This is all I have to give you. My breath, my life, my love, my Amy. Remember, when I give her to you, I am giving a part of myself. She may sound uncanny at times. She may behave childish. She may even act foolish. But she is my daughter, and time proves that you are meant to be together. Amy is a strong-willed, caring, and inquisitive young lady with a lot to say. Her cuddles not only soothe any soul but also support in dissipating the jabs that life throws at you. It's difficult to single out one thing I've discovered from her, but a few stand out: the importance of maintaining your brain active, staying curious about everything life has to offer, and being an independent, self-sufficient, and strong woman. More of a mentor to me.

Now there is you, to love her, to cherish her, as someone she can turn to. I wish happiness to both of you. You are now part of us and I am proud to call you, my son. Be blessed joy in abundance, be blessed with love immense. Let the two beautiful hearts of yours join to become one.

Dear son, marriage is a promise, a promise of lifelong friendship, a promise that you both accept each other with all your shortcomings, a promise that you both will share all your happiness and sorrows. Communication matters a lot. Whatever both of your moods are, open up. Listening each other non-judgmentally and speaking your heart out, is enough to resolve any problem.

With loads of love
Amma

Fragrance Of Five Elements

"No matter where i go, i still end up me. What's missing never changes. The scenery may change, but I'm still the same incomplete person. The same missing elements torture me with a hunger that i can never satisfy. I think that lack itself is as close as i'll come to defining myself." ~ Haruki Murakami

This book, I know, is incomplete. Because no mother can ever express all her emotions to her children through words. I may add on more and more to it as long as I am alive and after. Many more mothers may also add on to it. Thus, this may grow transcending time and period. Beyond ages and ages. I pray, like the smell of old books, let these words of your aging Amma too, lure you to unknown realms of joy and wonder.

I am quite aware that your days and nights revolve around quite a few of us. Your dreams, thoughts, aspirations, apprehensions, all orbit around a tiny world of us. Now you have added a handful of people more to this little world of yours; Your favourite people. As years go by let you be able expand your circle of favorites. Amma will be here extending my looks to your door steps, wherever you are. You can always lean on this sacred ring of bonding between the two of us.

As a beginning note, let me share the take away tips:

Dear daughter, you are strong, and you have all the potential, greatness, goodness and virtue within you. You are pretty, bold, and intelligent. You have wings and you are supposed to fly. Get out of your comfort zone, and be prepared to accept risks in life. Keep trying, hold on. Self-introspect, and be aware of yourself. Boost your body and mind with good thoughts, and your favourite hobbies and passions. Be patient and tolerant. Have control over your words and emotions. Have immense belief in your abilities. Keep your head high. Amidst all the Chaos, keep calm, and also keep your sense of humour alive. Listen, but take in only what is needed. Be touched by only the goodness in others. Manifest only the positives. Find happiness in little wonders of life. Keep the balance, Keep smiling, and move on. 'Coz, you know sweetheart, Life isn't easy, but it is damn beautiful. So spent every day living life to the fullest. It's a wonderful journey. But it doesn't mean you always wake up eager to embrace the day; you may feel exhausted. So sometimes you need to remind yourself that life is a wonderful gift. Live it to the lees.

"Dumbledore watched her fly away, and as her silvery glow faded, he turned back to Snape, and his eyes were full of tears.

"After all this time?"

"Always," said Snape.

This story, your favourite, that revolves around "Always" tell us, love make us to do great things. Love, and you live. Yes, real love exists and is immortal. It's profound and only you can give meaning to it. So here is Amma always wishing that you create YOU, in days to come...

Always.

Amma.

***

About the Author

Jyotsna P Katayaprath

Jyotsna P Katayaprath is a Creative Writer and translator. She writes both in English and Malayalam. Her first book of poems, "Ashes for yester years- Revelations of an Indian woman, was published by Penguin random house, Partridge publishing. Her second collection, I'm not just a body- Revelations of an Indian woman 11 was published by Author press, New Delhi. This collection has also won her "Poet of the Year" award by Ukiyoto publishers in the year 2022. She had also dealt with a column 'Literary Beat' in Kerala Calling by IPRD, Govt. Of Kerala. With a flair for innovative teaching and psychological counselling for teenagers, she has been a successful

English Language Teacher for more than two decades.